Taking our love offline

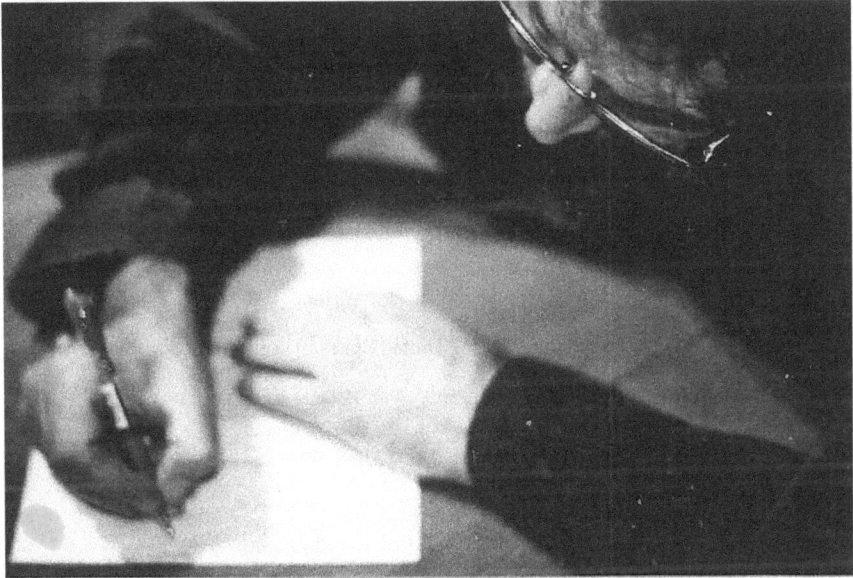

Poems by

Chuck Wanager

Ⅶ

Vabella Publishing
P.O. Box 1052
Carrollton, Georgia 30112
www.vabella.com

Manufactured in the United States of America

ISBN 978-1-938230-79-0

Library of Congress Control Number 2014919954

10 9 8 7 6 5 4 3 2 1

Taking our love offline

Poems

by

Chuck
Wanager

Also by Chuck Wanager

Prose

Jackson Flats
a novel

This collection of poetry is dedicated to my parents, Charlie and Joan, who gave me flight, and to those whose gracious help made this publication possible, Eleanor Hoomes, Bob Covel and other kindred souls in the Just Poetry group of the Carrollton Creative Writers Club.

Table of contents

I

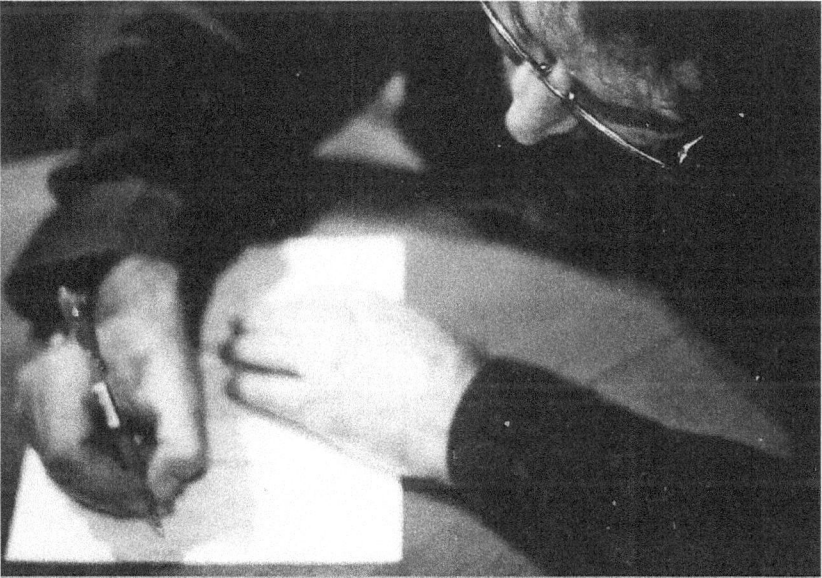

Taking our love offline

Love makes poets of us all,
the great philosopher said so
yeah, let's go then, you and I,
and write our poem on the
morning sky, where dawn
comes up like fire on our hearts,
licking, popping, sting/slapping.

The Internet is too small,
short, camped, virtual, ~~blurred~~
tame, blamed, defamed for our love.
Let's live raw in the un – polished,
un – disciplined, de – programmed.
Let's have life-on-the-run,
Recharging-our-love-as-we-go.

Let's go where we can see with
actionable rods, not through activated
ions; where I can see in 3-D and you, too,
and we ain't no holograms –
I'm hollerin' no!

I don't want your run-around,
I don't want your sister's photo
or one of you years ago.
I don't want your marketing
lines, frown lines or junk.

Let's ditch user names
forged addresses, copied photos
of places you've supposedly been,
counterfeit profiles, sham guyfriends –
all a phoney you. All to fake me.
That's all I ask. No fake you.

I txted her 2day

Txting –
what an abbreviated
world for the brave
we live in

Txting –
as in, I txted
her 2day,
wrote to say
wywh   (Wish you were here)

N2 tell her
ily and mhoty   (I love you and my hat's off to you)
and 2 say np   (no problem)
and u r so gr8!   (You are so great!)

Wrote with
tlc 2 my   (Tender loving care)
bff fwiw   (Best friend forever, for what it's worth)

N2 say again: (And to)

H = How r u?
E = Everything ok
L = Like to c u
L = Love 2 hear from u
O = Obviously I Miss U!

She txted back:
DILLIGAS   (Do I look like I give a shit?)

Pretty face

Pretty face, pretty face,
very pretty pretty face,
yes, yes, pretty face,
pretty face, lovely face,
yes, yes, love that face.

Ugly face, ugly face,
damn ugly ugly face,
no, no ugly face,
butt ugly ugly face,
no, no, skip that face.

Click, click, click, click,
click, click, click the face,
click, click, click, click
all manner of faces
on the dating places.

Pretty face, ugly soul,
how am I to know?
Ugly face, pretty soul,
but how can I be sure?
Ugly soul, pretty soul,
pretty face, ugly face?

Pretty face, pretty soul,
pretty soul, pretty face,
of course I would save you,
but what if there are none to click
on the dating places?

Pretty in or ugly out,
and vice versa, too,
stop dithering and select.
So, I try a common trick
and glance at her profile –
it's supposed to help.

Ugly profile,
click, click
find another place – quick!

Sunday evenings, late summer

Spread out now,
long and smooth
on grass close-cropped and
astringent with fresh-cut musk,
the blanket, and Mom and aunt
and Grandma H. and
older brother and cousin
plop down and lawn chairs
form a perimeter with grandpa
and Dad and uncle in those
and me and brother and
Grandma W. too and she rubs
my brother's back, her
hand up under his T-shirt with it all
rucked up, and him silent for
a long time, he's like that –
silent _____.
and Grandma H. sets off
telling one of her stories of
childhood on the farm
like falling in a well
cicada sending up
a crescendo and darkness coming
on and aunt cackles
and everybody chuckles
at her cackle, and all around
filling in lamp black and then
the flickering – undulating and
beckoning. And I and my brothers
would be up chasing, catching
them and someone would
yell, here! put them in this jar
and we can make a lantern!
and I would and glance at my
hands and there would be
the rub off on me
my self turned luminary.

Tinsel placers

Our neat tree
mocked those
with tinsel tossed
in happy disarray.

Not for us
to fling handfuls.
"Not natural!"
This tree? Said we.

"Every silvery strand
must be draped in
perfect place" astride
still-breathing boughs!

But now, when
placed together,
we go mute,
except for tinsel.

A Hobbit for the Holidays in 3-D!

Yeah, okay, if you can't,
don't. Look, don't try to come
if you truly can't, okay? I've
been there; I'll be fine right here.

"Take care of
your wife and her family.
You like your mother-in-law,
she's has been good to you.

"Oh, yeah, don't worry about that.
I'll get up late, eat great,
maybe go to church and sing
those Christmas hymns I like.

"Yeah, you know, and maybe
catch a matinee of 'The Hobbit.'
And it's in 3-D! Ok, and, oh,
Merry Christmas, son! Bye!

"Well, Caesar, it's you and me
for the holidays. We've been here
before, haven't we? Aw, stop your
squawking, we'll be fine.

"Yeah, we can eat what we want.
You get that great bird treat,
and I can have steak or chicken
or Tacos, not Pilgrim food."

Later:

"Hey, bird, I'm off!
Wait, I can't go.
I'll never see the movie,
it will be blurred in 3-D, too."

II

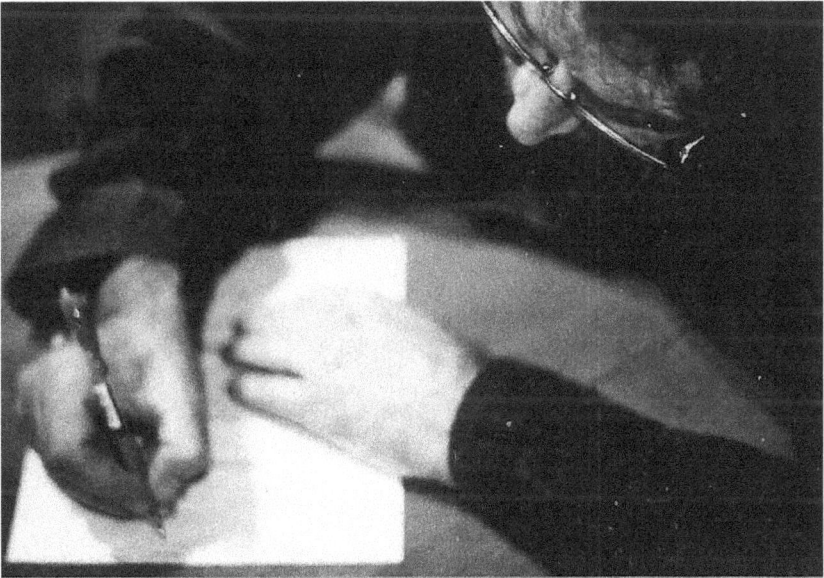

He turns to view it now

Whatever it is on the porch,
calm/settled, anchored there,
disappears as he rushes by,
Nikes tightly tied, jogging
togs securely hiked at waist,
those are important, can't wait.

Whatever it is catches his eye,
or, rather, this time, a glance
from an orbit's periphery,
what is it, he wonders,
like a sentinel's steady image
on the landing passing by?

Whatever it is sitting watch,
a plant, a chair, a desk to repair?
An old TV, a rug pushed back,
he turns to view it now
the porch at the end of his
run at the end of his day.

Whatever he passes, his heart
shifts to beating fast. But is
this too fast? He returns
carefully, and across the street
closely eyes the front of
the apartment, windows sealed.

Whenever in the past he's checked
there's nothing there, no chair,
potted plant, college flag, no dog nor cat.
Now, he studies, brows furrowed,
gets his answer cloaked in double knit.
He runs on, heart neatly beating.

Going places

God, I want to go places,
far, wide and set places,
green-white, battery-powered,
God-knows-where places,
places within paces
of me.

Black places, light places
watery, dry or deep places,
up and down, right or wrong,
marked, loose or tight places,
places with new faces
of me.

Old faces, you faces,
yellow-brown digital faces,
long, back-chinned, renovated
faces I make at places
totally disgusting
to me.

Cool places, creepy places,
sandy, public or hard places,
digging, nesting, growing,
gloomy dark places
spreading despair
in me.

Stormy places, shelter places,
soporific, underhanded places,
run and jump, push and shove
smelly-clean, unrestricted places,
places with mercy
for me.

Sand flea places,
portrait-painting places,
sunny, Sunday meeting,
rocky, white-foam places,
places without traces
of me.

Towed Away

Wait too long
stay too long
love too long
live too long
before too long
towed away.

Cross the law
cross the line
cross yourself
but not too long,
cross your streams,
cross it off,
blown away.

Walk across
sign the cross
love the cross
but live too cross,
kneel and cross
or turned away.

Towed away?
Stow away.
Come what may,
fight to stay.

Live to be
live to love
live the warning
when to cross
cross when read
return what's due
or duly towed away.

learn to wait,
wait to give,
wait to live,
then wait to wait,
but wait too late,
nonreturnable –
keep your fate.

Flat ain't cool

Flat ain't cool.
It ain't high up
like good luck.

It's low down
like the ground,
like dust – ground
down ground.

Not only that but its
big, wide-ocean flat
or like a swamp or like that,
but only and all ways flat,
which ain't cool.

Land may be
called prairie
but that's a trick,
you don't want to tarry
along a line that goes
flat, like dreams, in time.

You've seen
photos printed in 2-D,
seeing a place not to be.
Or even maybe gotten
up close to it – crept up
to that place where you'll see
you'll never sweat *this* geography.

If you've
done that –
gone up against the flat
– you wouldn't soon
forget its geology.
Dirt ready for framing,
which people from outside
think is cool; but it ain't that ….
It's flat.

Great for rearing
cattle or fat-hinnied hogs,
or flatulent people
who marvel at the marbled fat
from all that flat that
(we know) ain't really cool.

Still, people go fatuous
like a god came down and
dumped for us big bags
of potting soil on leveled land
that once was footing for
standout things, at least.

Planed earth
overflowed with
blues and reds and
bottles and stars
with yellows and pinks and
tall stems winking for miles.

Now its green and gold
in a square dance,
green on gold or gold on green
and a dusting on top as
golden kernels grow in bushels cubed
of today's prized prairie grass.

Me and friends back then,
we knew what it was like.
This place is a total bore,
we'd chant or sneer at
farmers with foreheads
of white crescents and spout:
When I get out of this damn place
I want to go to where there's nothing
like here.

Go to mountains dominant
with running, dangerous ridges;
roaring rabid waters, oceans
to give me body shivers
or hills of emerald dragon backs.

So, it was a joke, really,
we would smile thinly –
shoots flexed against
an ever-fallow horizon.
We were always thinking up
with wispy contrails spiking.

We'd get away;
we'd see to that – just wait.

Little White House, Warm Springs, Ga.

No relief from the heat,
his heat, while I eat,
where he ate,
sitting in the sky,
cliff high.
I see him eating from an auto seat,
window down, Big Flap intruding.

I sit where maybe he sat
while his thoughts meld with mine
to rise on afternoon thermals and circle –
guns, tanks, darkness, mushrooming
death shooting down our idyl;
flags flash crooked symbols,
people, crossed lives.

But I can't think of those
like he did;
He thought big and made them live,
and the world watched, too.

I walk where he rolled,
spirit buoyed in heated waters,
and bend to play with
a little dog ... And talk on those
clunky phones, and hope for the hopeless,
and feel my pain ease with his.

No relief from the heat
as I drive back on
my road, not his.
A truck passes with
flags flapping, crossed symbols
and stars that rise.

And I see him, torso and head
too big, encompassing cockpit,
face to the sun, hat brim a-flip
a gesture of jauntiness,
a smile for the wind.

Your particular genius

Find your
area of particular genius, said Infomercial Man.

What if:
your particular genius is collecting trash?
repairing walkmans?
causing trouble?
writing poetry?
doing this?

How do
you find your area of particular genius?

Like this?
Take a Cosmo quiz?
Spend all your life at one thing
and all your money trying different things?
Follow your hands?
Your eyes or ears?
Calmly begin zazen and download intuition?

Oh, I know, here's how:
Listen to the guy on TV:
Take heed:

"Yes, call now at KNOW-GENIUS. We have a whole
professional staff just waiting to take your call. Call us today, at
K-N-O-W-G-E-N-I-U-S! Remember, you get the Know-Your-
Genuis kit, which regularly retails for $99.95, plus the two-page
booklet that tells you how to use your kit to find your particular
genius! Truly a gift to you!

"This offer only good where legal in the United States and
Canada. Know your genius today!

"This has been a paid commercial announcement. Views expressed are not particularly from any area of genius."

III

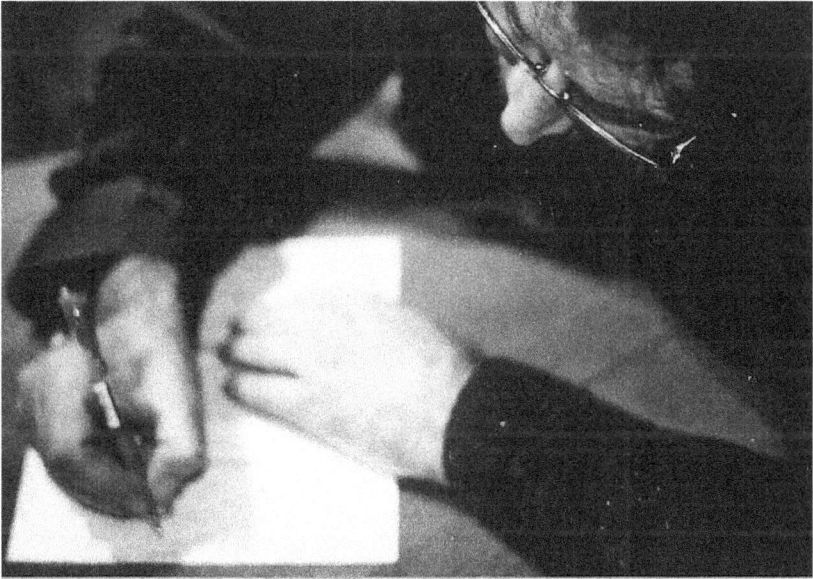

III

Like Lincoln

When I was a child
I wanted to be like him, like Lincoln.
I lived on the prairie, near where he lived;
I stared out my bedroom window to see his home.

He was great --
Jesus, what a man!
I would be great, too. I prayed
to God and stood on a book to be tall.

His IQ spiked the charts
so I thought big thoughts,
talked big talk. He was humble
and I was too, to be like Lincoln.

He was homely, ugly even,
people said, and he did, too!
I grew angry for him. I said: Hell
with blemishes! He looked like, well, Lincoln.

He grew inward
when depressed. So, I
tucked into a ball, shook, slurred
my words, four score and more.

Then mom said,
c'mon boy, you'd better be better,
got to do more, more, more and more!
Wouldn't it be great to be like Lincoln?

No, mom, I wrote
on back of an envelope;
I am too much like him,
warts, melancholia and all,
way too much like Lincoln.

Like Lincoln? Not him

Lincoln? What a joke,
a letter to an editor read,
which made me wonder,
he said that and this is today?

As I read, bile flowed, exploded:
Union soldiers (those blue bellies)
we think of them as heroes? Ha!
"Barbarians," they ruined his South.

"All true Southerners,"
(And certainly he was
one), "glory in the
deaths of every last one of them."

Many Americans buy
one heck of a great big lie.
Because naively they believe
in a righteous Northern cause.

Just like in our colonies,
they sought only to "freely
leave" what they had "freely joined,"
thank you, ma'am, no harm intended.

"Unfortunately, a tyrant"
prowled White House floors,
"resolved" to gut the league
and lay it prostrate under foot.

Ah, but "fortunately" that big
bully got what he "richly deserved,"
and letter writer wished he had
been in the balcony that night.

"So I could have reached
down, stuck my finger in
his wound and see if I
could have made him twitch."

Like Jesus

When I was a child
I prayed to be like Jesus
that would have made me famous
and helped me win friends, too.

To be Jesus Jr.
that would have been super!
I would have eased all pain
and made all life worth the dying.

I wanted to be him
then I heard how he died.
Damn. I really don't want to
be too much like him, not like that.
Jesus!

Like Big Sur

You are like Big Sur to me,
holding me in your
    power
    just as that mystic
land hugs a shrouded sea

Like sun-tanned sand
your hair
    spilling
    over me,
streaming ready access

Far down on beaches
barking – waves
    lapping
    at your side
to slip sensuously away

Over Bixby Bridge,
tested through ages
    and high winds
    to span the gap
of our existence

Up the road vectoring
    high from my crossing
    carrying me where
dreams build trestles
in impromptu time

Red skin rising

Red skin rising
mounts lesions of despair,
like a blotch on bark,
raising questions –
something so largely there
could mark us like that?

It's a ring
of human bondage
preying specially
on crippled DNA,
the young, the me.

Mom thought
it from spider bite
and so my hopes had gone ….

Now after years
of tar and needles
shrink wrap and mercury,
mean chemistry and reeking
shampoos, bland meals
and yeast meant for cakes,
sun and sweat and fears

The pain, the sickness
the sights and stares
the pointed questions
the dread of loving
and loathing linger.

Sometimes – it's gone
with the weather
or a slip into
humidified climes.

Ah, but then I wonder,
if you're truly gone,
my old lichen,
what happens to the tree?

Gun play

Gun gone

Gun! grandpa's gun! grasp the case and pull it out while gettin' up gambit grows. All guile, gall and gravitas, a guise for all the gullible, but then a gutsy guard with a Glock goes grim, gut-grazed. And gonzo gunfire leaves gauzy gusts, gushing gore and our gun-shy genesis, gamboling, grasping, too soon gone. The gruesome gamble yields only gelded glory as gaunt, gloomy groups grieve by tiny gra-ves. They are now the gut shot.

HeHateMe

HeHateMe
said the back
of the football jersey.

I wonder.
I don't hate he,
but maybe he does hate me.

Or would
hate me, like
thee hate me, sometimes.

Actually, thee
hate me most of the time,
like he apparently hate me other times.

And often,
along with me,
thee would probably hate he.

But most
times, he and me hate
thee, through and through,

Like, sometimes,
MeHateMe.

In my work

"This is good,
This is damn good!"
A club member said. Others, too,
in kind mode licked my ego,
stroked my morale, sent me
to my feel-good place.

They actually said it! God,
how I liked it! I really loved
it! Filed away: share
and help, salve and soothe.
Now precious succor to me.

Work was never
like this! Never!
In my work, while I worked,
it was ever: "What the hell?
That bastard's getting ahead of me!
That's not fair! Nor just! Unkind!"

Fight back – scratch and grab!
Take that, and that, you f-ing jerk!
back bite, bite back,
stab in front n' then the rear,
kick him in his ego! Hurt
his feelings, make *him* bleed,
cut *his* emotions red and raw!

Pat, tap or balm?
Are you kiddin'? More like
grumble n' grouse, fear n' spit;
glare n' point, cut n' slice,
"Get the hell outta here!"

But this group, what nirvana!
No cancerous bicker
or backbite, sabotage or hate.
But an infectious light
that lengthens n' widens,
brightens n' sharpens,
reveals n' most often, remains.

"I like that," the woman said.
I like her and the others for liking my work.
Not necessarily because it is good, but because it's good to hear.

IV

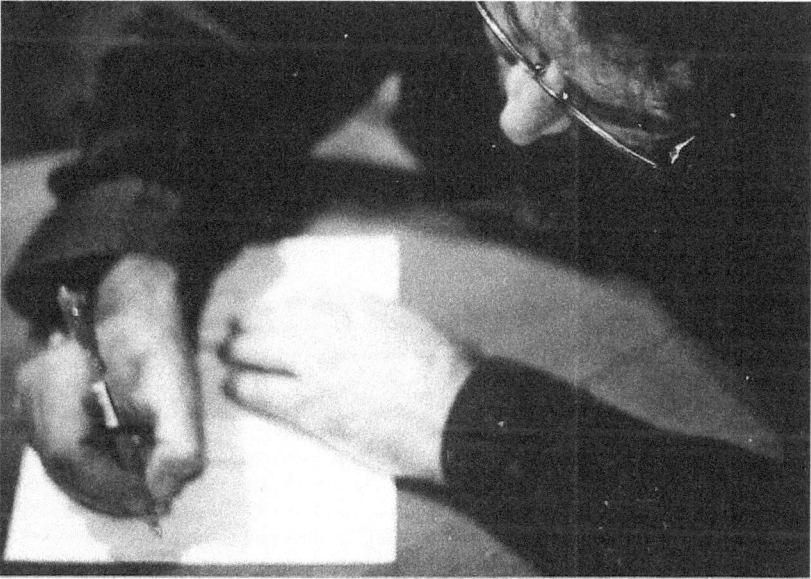

I feel eyes

Often when I
gaze into center
black I can't hold
my center back

Cold rush
shakes flesh and
verve, spinning all
to deepening dark

Jumbled landing
triggers painful warning
another mind has scanned
mine and found it lacking

Stock defenses
spring too late. I slouch
toward soundness seeking
shelter in luxurious fatigue

Ode to rock 'n' roll

Tornadoes blew
in Telestar on that
trip to Chicago when you
went platinum with a bullet

In that cold November
sweaty-palmed youth pressed close
discovering gender glances
while you ignited the minutes
and rocked my soul with chances

You captured our movements
like those of a first-time dancer
and even found the right note
to fill my veins with spurs

Now, the beat has changed
We speak of age, and
burs become a velvet
cloth brushing
quick across my heart

Loneliness sucks

Like this page
with nothing on it
no writing, not perforated
no smudges

A tree
abducted, stripped
cut, diced
drowned, bleached

till lost
nothing at all
a seed never
planted

Wasting time

Hours don't rhyme,
poems don't make sense,
it's just a mass of dithering,
can anything be claimed today?
Wasting too much time.

I'm missing every uplink
through clicks out of sync
as a warning buoy flashes,
your sand's running out, dude,
and here you are sifting it.

Coke!

O Lord, our Lord,
I love coke.

O Lord, wow Lord,
I want my coke.
No, I *have* to *have* coke.

Yes! Sure, I need more.
Get up, ingest, infuse, go to bed – coke.
Cool up, scarf up, stoke up – coke.

O Lord, my Lord,
Give me that coke.
the ever pick-me-up,
the always-get-me-up,
my addiction.

You're not a pretty white,
you turn my teeth brown
and you burn going down,
but I still-must-have you,
coke.

Coca-Cola,
Co-Colas,
Coke, Coke and more Coke.
fizz up, power up,
My God! Gotta have my Coke.

The Necklace

Here comes that funky one
she has a new necklace
I saw it on her today

She was gone
and then she
was wearing *that*

How strange it was
leathery and shiny
with a wire sticking out

What does she think, it's great?
She struts around here
and now she has that thing

I don't like it
I stay away from her
it smells of humans

What kind of guy?

What kind of lover
is that guy?

Is he an
asshole or what?

Is he better
than me?

Found a
photo of him –

Hmm
nope. Not
that I can see.

Depression cuts dull

No, it
doesn't bother
calling or texting
or sending courtesy mails.

My altered
ego just appears,
as you might guess,
a visitor adept at sabotage.

It cuts
jagged, like a rusty razor
in sex, with bite and pull,
not smooth, not wet; eviscerating lovers.

Or it
tears like a tumbling slug
through stringy muscle, ripping
and gouging, splatting rich blood.

Or catches
and clings to my being
like a hard, lumpy stool,
not in or out, not about to move.

Weighing
on my brain like a tumor,
black, heavy, thudding like
a ceaseless pounding sledge.

Stealing
my joy, all joy,
like a thief while on vacation
for fun long and way overdue.

Smashes
like a train
smearing me all
over the track, smacking, clubbing,
shattering confidence like blown glass.

Blocking
my music, my rocking
dance, locking each easy step,
a slow stumble to dazed dependence.

Addling
me my mind with d-d-doubt,
d-d-distracting me, s-s-scrambling
me my thoughts, crashing my my system.

Till
I am left with
ajoohmoo. As it has been with them,
a plunge too deep, to ah-emmmmm.

Hahooom,
hahdaroom? Are that
to me? No, wait! I ca – ,
I can do this; I can do this ....

Yes.
Depression cuts dull,
steadily severing the sum of me
until I want a knife that's sharp.

But, hey,
I over-dramatize, right? It's not
really that bad, mumble/crying,
foundering/feeling stuck, not in, not out.

When terrorism strikes

Break out toxic
detection crews,
denounce all your vices
when terrorism strikes.

A plane or two may upend,
or plague or blight descend,
from Mideast to London or here,
But, hey, many may cheer
when they see you run to hiding.

A pipe bomb or
pressure-cooker type
may target those
blindly passing them by.

Or after shopping,
your chicken may
explode from meta data
or dirty bomb exposure.

But rest assured,
we'll run and shout
and call out the FBI, ATF,
and First Division, too.

And if the level goes
to red, all work and
play will tremble to halt,
but have a good flight to you and yours!

Boom!

Boom – boom – boom – pa-boom!
Huh, oh, here it comes
Boom, boom, thump pa-thump!
Oh, God, we know that score

Hear? It's not Mozart magic
nor lulling nudge from Brahms
no, you can't shake this pulsing
blast of the new urban thunder!

Bam-bam-bam sha-bam!
A nightmarish pounding
slackening smiles, bones and hair,
a trillion cells ajar; DNA in death spiral

Feel it? Feel it thump?
Do you feel that whump?
A volume-totally-cranked
Boom! Thump! Thud! Pa-Thud?

Even Earth trembles 'n rocks
high on anxiety's scale
rhythmic waves bam 'n wham
thank you much, enjoyed it, ma'am

Hear it getting close?
Thump! – Thud! – Thump! – Sha-thud!
Here audio blasts roam
in an ever-widening arc

See it? See my house
shimmy? windows rattle
walls reverb-erate
with Bam-tttllle! Ram-tttlle!

Whump! Sub-woofer bass
from way-deep throat
addles thoughts as it – bam!
Rolls mossy stones away!

Ever on it goes
future frozen in predatory blows.
Roll over fat man 'n little boy
meet the new Big Boom

It's our noise embolism
our soul's terror. No need
for bullets when boom
boom! Boom! Thunders by

V

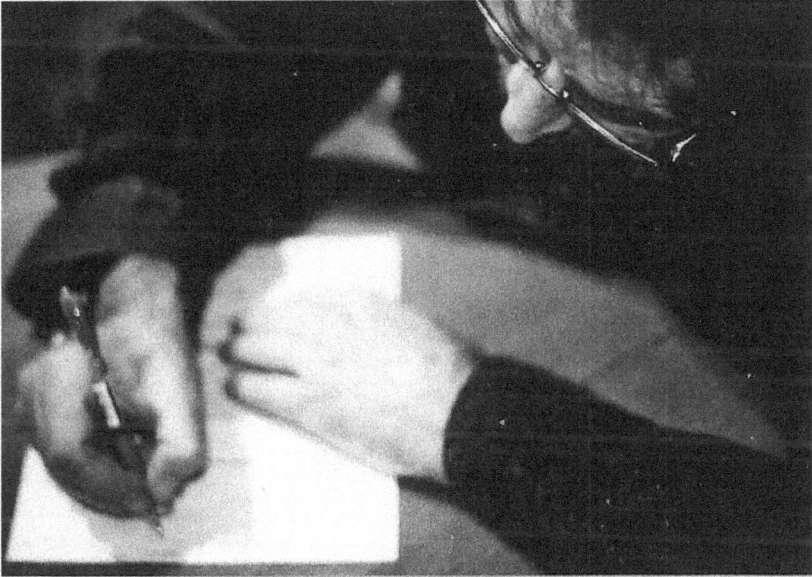

Titus and his clan
(Sung to the tune of Itsy Bitsy Spider)

Titus & his gorilla clan
climbed up the mountain top

'Round came their kin
and blew the clan apart

Out came the guards
and told the brutes to stop!

But Titus & his clan
ne're climbed the mount again

Birds to me

Dazzled heads, feathered debris,
stalking ancient Greek lands,
muddling gravity.

Wings on a cloud brighten
by-gone stage, a fluttering muse
to the bards.

Apple trees lost in flight
await soaring drones
with flashing beaks.
.

But we don't need that,
not for our soul's delight,
the birds.

Twitters descended from
lizard's roar, pump our spirits,
vent our souls.

Thrills, trills, brilliance flashing,
fibrous shafts conjuring indigo
undulate our days.

Even the vulture,
scanning from on wing,
readies our way.

Stuffedbirds

Fans to cool,
can't cool to-be roasters,
hot wings, drums, necks and nuggets,
        stacked in steel.

Once snow-white
birds CrammedInCages;
youthful broilers boiling in
        summer heat.

Now ill-fated freight,
they travel tightly tucked in big rigs,
feet flailing, necks recoiling from acrid air;
        eyes ammonia-seared, flat.

Genetic freaks,
tweaked for people pleasure,
with breasts and thighs overly endowed,
        crouch and hobble, painfully lame.

Fusty chattel,
closed off, closeUp, can't
climb out; reared in near darkness on
        manure-tainted beds.

Foul digs
attract assailant salmonella and crony
campylobacter; disorders of blood and guts, and
        those that slowly suffocate.

Stressed out,
mussed up, gust-locked
creatures to be gutted, caught in
        cages guttated.

Shocked,
hot-frocked, once endlessly cackling,
but now stuffing sound, they bound down
        white-lined highways.

Shedding
sweet snow, dropped in desperate
flakes, somber, shifting about, fine feathered
        clemency calls.

Abruptly,
their big-wheeled vessel veers,
sideways shooting white-hot messages
        into the air.

Fragile
missives float loose, light,
tumble and turn, free to find
        windshields, ground.

They land
on ears of lead,
unheeded distress signals from
        CrammedUpBirds good as dead.

The escape

Stuck in truck
in major funk,
broilers rasped and heaved;
"forget the cooking,"
said a man in muddy overalls

"They're already broiled,"
said the man at the door
who came in on the truck.
"Several of those birds
are now long departed"

He nodded to the spot
where the long, low
rig had skidded to a stop
where a man now
counted cages, grim and gray

All scooted
all around, super
hot and crowded
there in the truck,
bleak birds now aboard

Away they all flew,
and then a fryer
got stuck amid wire
in the truck heading to
her disjointing, so humane

Crunched up, hot
bird peeked for way out
One bird pecked, feathers
flew, and saw – a chink

Flee, get gone!
She pulled and pushed
and cartwheeling out,
fell in a fully targeted zone

Quick, look out!
She zigged and zagged,
and jumped and flicked
as traffic zoomed and missed.

And missed again
as she capered and
ducked and dinked
— and flew

And we all knew
she could — a little

Is it strangely me?

Is it strangely me?
A time machine, the tree,
taking me back to play
under its emerald canopy.
The tree I see still
the size as then,
and now I see – a friend?

More so than that,
a kindly family member – a
grandmother or, perhaps, father?
Want to say hello, go
up to it, hug it around the neck.
How strange to be?

Of course, the tree
can't see or hear me.
Why do we love it so?
Why do we cling to it,
fight to have it around?

It alloys oxygen, yes,
and makes big shade
in deep hot July,
and beckons in the distance
when work is fully done.
But why do people say,
we shouldn't let it go?

It's a friend you can't buy
these days. A friend of deep
roots; a staunch, determined,
tough-skinned friend.

A friend to the
climate changed, mud and dirt,
cheap apartmented, parking
lotted, development dotted,
deep dark end.

Dogwood king

When I enter
late afternoon,
dogwoods in wild
woodlot besiege me.
A burst of pink on white,
heralding spring rising. White
shrapnel on downy breeze.

Dogwood,
king of the wood,
crowned in April,
multi-hued month,
king season in South,
brilliant minions escaping.

I stand back
as niche lights up,
blazes in a blinking, then
fades white; from light,
brilliant pinks; to shade,
reds all aflame.
Mallow blossoms, desiring light,
go fallow for green.

So happy together

Imagine me and you I do
I think about you day and night
It's only right
to think about the one you like
and hold it tight
so happy together ....
        – with apologies to The Turtles

Turtles
Peanut Butter and Jelly
       stuck at the shell,
carapace to carapace
they were hooked,
       Jelly never righted.

Life to life,
       day to day,
year to year,
they shared
       always.

Other turtles said
       too bad,
they were uninvited twins
a burden to each other
       neither could unload.

But like
       standing stones
they walked strong
and when in storm were
       a rock against the wind.

When the dog
       wanted to tear them in two
the turtles turned

impenetrable nut
       the hound did eschew.

Maybe, after all, they
       were happy together
like rocking Flo and Eddie
of a much different
       turtle team.

But, like in the fable
       when they
wound up chased
would they ever
       win the race?

And would they
       ever know love?
What tortoise in its right
mind would want to marry
       two lumps in one?

When it came
       to traveling,
wasn't it Peanut Butter
that always hit the road?
       And feeding time? What to do?

Regardless, they galumphed on
       together forever,
come hare or high water,
in unhurried heaven
       or mutation hell.

Hide! Great blue island

Good God!
Great blue island,
go/run/hide in the
great blue deep-down
where we can't find you.

Plunge!
to bottomless reaches,
where trawlers, drones
or nautiluses buckle,
and darkness fills
voids like oil atomized.

Slip!
watery shelf, subducting
your stunning contours,
maxed out from minimal things,
stretched out for streamlining.

Sound Now!
Deep … deep … deep
↓

down
↓

down
↓

down

↓

down

↓

↓

down
to unfathomable reaches.

Go!
before niggling creatures
with great big grey matter –
the max blood or oil or
electron has pulsed
– run you to ground
all of you, an archipelago of pain.

Hide!
before the stalkers
slice you like cheese logs
into ribbons of
Grade-A blubber
and render you a
natural Bonny (blue) Light.

Run silent, run far!
and wait till those
with great intellect are rotted.
Or conjure yourself gone,
melding while you can with
engulfing blue.

Or morph to dark energy
floating by as we search
for you in some forgotten
wintering grounds. Flip your
tail and porpoise with our brains.

VI

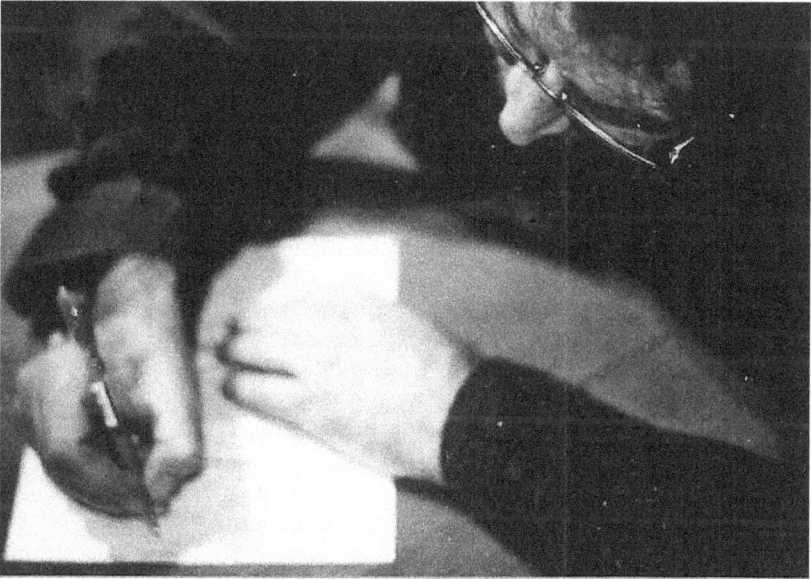

IV

Sign on a tree, a dream fragment

Sitting in peace at a nearby
food processing plant,
a tree along a fence,
a bird's song frames real time.

I nod to my wife,
and rising out of my car,
see it:
a sign on a post
holding up the fence.

A hand nailed it there,
a message in a square,
aging white back contains black letters.
Rusted where bent at top,
and along bottom in parallelism.
I move close up, read:

>   test your Man
>   Hood
>   Join the Greatest Army
>   in History, join
>   the Army of Mars.

At home that night
I look up:
black sky back embraces white stars,
the most lustrous, Mars,
nearer now than 60,000 years.

So you can see it
capped up and down
in ice.
Ice – water – man?
An army of Mars.

Clock in, clock out

Clock in, clock out,
thunk, thunk, thunk,
that's the daily routine.
Knowing when our day
begins and when it ends,
once out of sync, you're fired.

Clock in, clock out,
smm-thenk,
smm-thenk, smm-thenk,
that's the respirator's routine.
Pumping air in and out,
keeping your heart dead on beat.
Lose that rhythm, you're expired.

Clock in, clock out,
boom, boom, boom,
that's the universal routine.
Spiraling in and massing out,
Move too fast, you're mired.

Mars from the upstairs window

She steps a
staircase to stars
spackeling the night,
waiting in the winking window.

She's climbed these stairs before,
pulled to the center of her universe,
where galactic chaos sent bodies in motion,
colliding in a spasm of screams and cascading noise.

She rose on the
horizon of her pulsing
nebula, her gravity sending
protostars squealing to their inert state.

Now, she ascends
in her well-worn vector
and through the upstairs window
sees Mars, closest in 60,000 years.

Though tired of stairs,
she ascends anyway, and is
reborn to a place where atoms
glide by atoms in orbits calmly revolving.

Purple blotches of the heart

I have seen them,
profuse splotches
tattooing skin,
tincture of time
in jarring hue –
an imperious purple.

Blotches,
I fear,
like sun spots,
reflecting trouble within.

Skin taut
like it'll tear
when she moves.
Shriveled, creased and crinkled,
corrugated air.
Translucent, like you can
see clean to the bone.

Bones like chicken bones,
thin, flimsy
like the marrow
could fling out.

Voice thin as skin,
scrambled phrases,
network clotted,
uplink fading.

Purple blotches,
the doctor says,
signal heart disease.
But she holds my hand,
emotion patching in,
transmitting strong ...

As dad lay dying

*Yes? Uh, yes, come in, what? Oh, Dad? He's there, yes,
that's right, he's dying*

*Look, he gasps, another fix, oxygen pumping
kaah!-aah, kaah!-aah, kaah!-aah, kaah!-aah, aah!-aah,
he gasps, face distorts, mouth gaping, toking life. Yes, that's
right, autonomic ... but barely.*

*Morphine dripping, no pain, I think, I hope. Body stirs, bed
engulfs it*

*The creature breathes with that call – kaah!-aah, kaah!-aah.
Air injected, but is it really alive? A gaunt cocoon, a mummy.
Kaah! - aah, kaah! - aah, it bleats, day after day.
That ...keeps it alive.*

*The insistence stops. Kaah! - aah, kaah! - aah, kaah! - aah,
ka .....*

*My brother wakes, no sound. He looks, shakes me.
Listen, he says ....
Yes ... yes.*

*It – he – is gone. Nurse steps over, lifts his hand, places index
finger to his wrist*

She nods.

VII

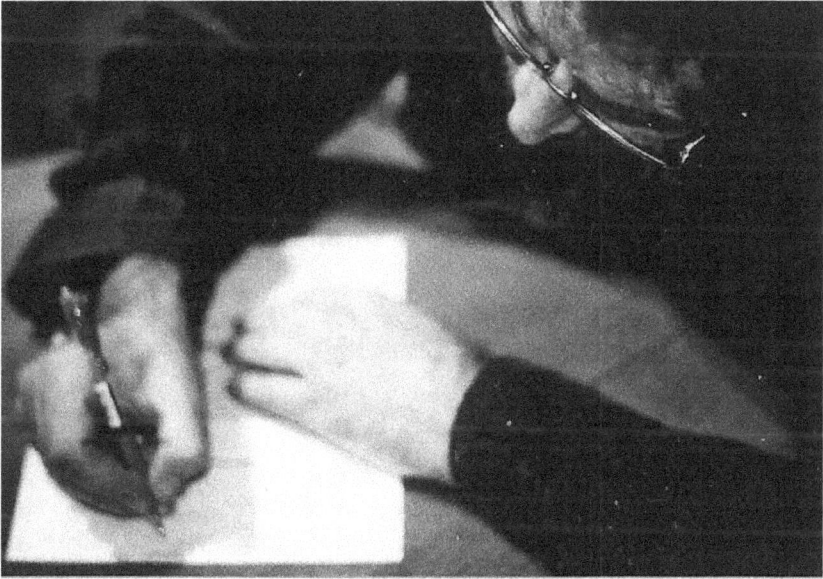

Somewhere in a parallel universe

Somewhere in a parallel universe,
maybe I'm young,

                                        strong,

                                        dark and
tall,

                                        killer
handsome,

                                    have cans larded
with money,

                                    have friends by the
hundreds,

                                    a handy Caribbean
laps at my door,

                                    my backyard mirrors
Myrtle Beach,

                                    I'm a huge success,

                                    I'm happy,

                                    I have you.

You have me in a parallel universe,   somewhere.

Born to Kill

Eyes shoot wide. Then
screaming, explosions.
"No! No!" Children,
teachers falling; blood splattering.

Cut –

Good evening from
the land of bouncy step,
straight teeth, expectant lives
n more dreams flushed in blood.

In our homes, streets,
schools, the cruel harvest
goes on, easily googled, easily cut,
easily pasted on intro-active hearts.

We remember kids
combined at a Colorado school,
those eight student nurses under
knife and prophetic tattoo.

A California man puts
a stop to five kids meals.
Atlanta and VTech and movie goers
n more n more dead n slain in piles of more.

As our gore and guts
copulation goes on, peace
must be resting somewhere –
on the other side? But when?

Remember the face
of Chicago's mass killer.
It might be right –
a pox corrodes our souls

As rhythm from hunting
days vibrates in our genes,
rendering us forever
born to kill – and kill.

Case No. 868

Jesus Manuel Daniel, No. 62355,
clambers into faux-paneled courtroom VIII,
standing accused of rendering a man to 0.
No. 62355 folds in his hands
at the end of 2 shackled arms.

He folds hands in again,
sits dazed and gazing at
District Judge No. 3,
all grim, glum and tight of mouth,
loosing black-robed, size-40 justice.

A blend
of Hispanic and black,
and no personal attorney in the mix,
No. 62355 stands 0 chance
in faux-paneled courtroom VIII.

"Well, he didn't give the victim 0
a chance!" the prosecutor cries.
Made him 0 in the flash of a 32,
all because 62355 got greedy
and cashed in my client!"

"It was self-defense,"
the public defender shouts.
"0 tried to make 62355 a 0 first!"

No. 62355 shuffles to
all grim and glum No. 3.
Would No. 62355
live in a cell, say No. 62,
the rest of his life?
Or come up a 0?

No. 62355 does 0,

except to fold in again,
sit and gaze while standing
accused of negation
in case No. 868.

No. 62355, you're a 0,
No. 3 says, and
throws back his
long, black size 40.

No 3 sentences No. 62355
to death; bottom line, a 0.
So, the score reads 0 to 0.

And case No. 868
ends up on shelf G
in big, sterile room F
with nothing positive for humanity.

I look down

I look down
one sock blue the other black
At least it isn't brown

Further down
treading the floor I find
the brown with matching black

Deep down
I want to laugh but not my ex
she will flash red and scream

Wake up, you dreamer
and get it right! Your
awareness is much too slight!

I look mid-way
pants blue shirt green
hey, at least I'm clean

I look out
at hands black and blue
from what I've been through

I look up
hair thinned to silver and brown
…. at least I'm still around

Along the road to Baghdad

God
damn,
I'm mad!
my dad was cut up bad,
then stuffed in a body bag,
along the road to Baghdad.

Tank
tagged my dad,
laid him flat as a desert slab,
another victim of deadly Jihad,
along the road to Baghdad.

God!
Dad,
a nomad,
who I saw only via iPad, was
extracted through freakin' Jalalabad,
his body stuck in that goddamn bag!
a long road from Baghdad.

VIII

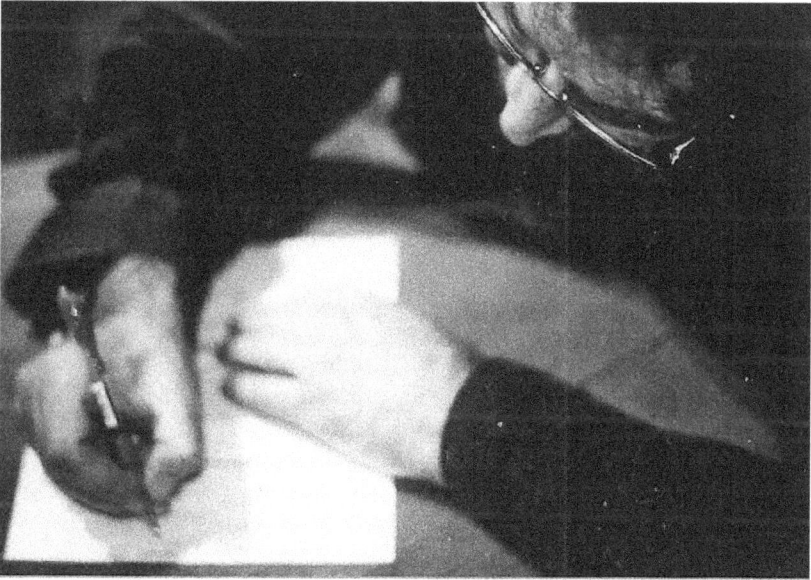

In fields, snow glistens

In autumn, egg-white,
luminous in early light,
slinking under bushes, hanging
around trees, clinging last thread.

Refugee from big trucks,
escapee from canvas caravan,
not tied down, free to drift, cloud
the road, seeking LZ near my home.

It's our lord, who
granted riches – for some –
bolls up from common
stock, clay, heat, sweat, rock.

four-starred, fluffy, linty,
plucked off, green all over,
a weevil sucking life,
blighting all tractable land.

Beyond fresh asphalt,
I gaze upon a gauzy specter,
a hunched black man, picking,
chopping. There comes a call.

Receive, voice, return,
a streaming chant loops forever.
It echos off glistening white mansions
and through glued-together boxed rot

In the fields, down
glistens in the heat of
shadow man's working beat.
Snow on sweaty skin
won't brush off.

Yule tide

Bright morning already
and the eager town recharges;
cars pull up while tractors tug
long, flat trailers, not yet all dressed out.

It's warm for December
as red sun rises above bare
limbs and fleshy knots shuffling
lawn chairs, blankets just right.

We await Yule tide's
flow down streets flanked by
blue cop rip-rap and yellow-ribboned
banks of psyched-up, dazed-out young.

Annexing asphalt,
they squat before aging elders
to fidget/wait for blimped-out mice,
big red trucks 'n cloying put-on faces.

My two young boys go
wide aperture with long looks
and shaded eyes, then tug, wiggle/shrug,
and finally find it hard to stay all in one place.

At route's head, by the Dairy
Queen, babbling, ready to go,
bands, tricked-out trailers and kin
pool and stream in meandering file.

Sirens yawp and jolt,
mounted tack glints and blinds
and Santa, floating by, defies gravity
as he guides a sleigh trussed on high.

Waves wash
over easy chairs and
way-up shoulder perches,
while a brassy silver bells wavers over all.

Chair jockeys rise
to applaud, and my face
flushes as my kids rush for candy
tossed to hundreds of grabbing hands.

But, wait ... what's this?
What are *they* doing here?
I go dazed. Fetid flotsam darkening
tide, sauntering all bunched up,
bearing unmistakeable ill.

Hoodless now, rough ranks
don street clothes in many colors
and shackles on their hearts. In silence, they
wave and acting big, scatter their toxin to the crowd.

They smile, a klan for the masses,
and all scurry for *their* treats. But I want
to shout: "Stop! Don't take that from *them!*"
They have robbed out warmth from this day.

But I don't yell, nor do I make
an obvious display of my emotion.
A stronger one grips me now: What if *they*,
breaking step, practice *their* violence on me?

As they pass, though, I relax.
Name and rep may rattle and scare
but I have gazed into their eyes.
Still, it's time to gather sons and go.

Next day, back at work,
while the specter hangs, scaring
up fears, worries and doubts, I do not
mention my own take on the jarring scene.

Then questions flow —
what did you do when you
saw *them*? Us? Well, we walked away.
Worried about you, your kids, they say.

Too much stuff!

Black plastic bags, 1, 2, 3,
tall, double strength and gator-locked
stuffed with frames, cards, clothes, pens
mine and collected with care

Slump plump at the door
ready for their final journey
plopped and tumbling over
bump, bump, bump on pickup palette

Squawk, and metal maw gapes,
flipped to flapping for its oblation,
photos, souvenirs, buttons, books
and tapes

The condiments of life

www.ingramcontent.com/pod-product-compliance
Lightning Source LLC
Chambersburg PA
CBHW060032050426
42448CB00012B/2974